PUFFIN BO

Sister Madg

About Sis

Sister Madge Mappin is a nun who lives in The Convent of Our Lady of Immense Proportions, in the Eltham hills. As a child Madge was always eager to perform good deeds, such as helping old people across the road, even when they didn't want to go. She pushed her grandmother around in a wheelbarrow for many years. There was no reason at all for this.

At the age of eighteen, Madge decided to become a nun because Jesus told her to. The careers counsellor told Madge to be a hairdresser, but Jesus won. Madge soon developed a talent for writing funny verses. Once she made the Mother Superior laugh so hard that the cigar fell out of her mouth and into her Ribena.

Sister Madge's first book, *Sister Madge's Book of Nuns*, was voted the best book in the entire history of the world by her grandmother, who was by now confined to the wheelbarrow and quite confused.

Now, sixteen years later, Sister Madge has created a special bumper version of her original masterpiece with twice as many nuns. And Puffin has printed it. This is what we call a miracle.

Other books by Doug MacLeod
and Craig Smith

The Birdsville Monster

Further titles by the same author and
illustrator to be published in the year 2307

Matthew, Mark, Luke and John,
Kindly Put Your Trousers On

The Amazing Adventures of
Prune Girl and Cheese Boy

Germs are Fun

My Brilliant Nose

The Magic Cat-litter Box

Finding Your Bottom

Sister Madge's Book of Nuns

Doug MacLeod

Illustrated by

Craig Smith

PUFFIN BOOKS

The author and illustrator would like to express their thanks to Jane Covernton

Puffin Books

Penguin Books Australia Ltd
250 Camberwell Road
Camberwell, Victoria 3124, Australia
The Penguin Group
80 Strand, London WC2R ORL, England
Penguin Putnam Inc.
375 Hudson Street, New York, New York 10014, USA
Penguin Books Canada Limited
10 Alcorn Avenue, Toronto, Ontario, Canada, M4V 3B2
Penguin Books (N.Z.) Ltd
Cnr Rosedale and Airborne Roads, Albany, Auckland, New Zealand
Penguin Books (South Africa) (Pty) Ltd
24 Sturdee Avenue, Rosebank, Johannesburg 2196, South Africa
Penguin Books India (P) Ltd
11, Community Centre, Panchsheel Park, New Delhi, 110 017, India

First published by Penguin Books Australia, 2002

Original edition published by Omnibus Books, 1986

1 3 5 7 9 10 8 6 4 2

Designed by Karen Trump, Penguin Design Studio
Typeset in 12/14pt New Baskerville by Post Pre-press Group
Printed and bound in Australia by
McPherson's Printing Group, Maryborough, Victoria

National Library of Australia
Cataloguing-in-Publication data:

MacLeod, Doug, 1959–.
Sister Madge's book of nuns.

New ed.
ISBN 0 14 330014 8.

1. Nuns – Juvenile poetry. 2. Children's poetry, Australian. 3. Humorous poetry, Australian. I. Smith, Craig, 1955–. II. Title

A821.3

www.puffin.com.au

For St Stephen

Contents

The Bumper Book of Nuns *1*

Sister Brock and Our Lady of Immense Proportions *3*

Sister Flo and the Vegies *9*

Sister Stephanie and the Gang *12*

Sister Bossy and the Angel *17*

Sister Poppy and the Plague *20*

Sister Isobel and the Zoo *23*

Sister Christabel and the Cushion of Joy *28*

Sister Joss and the Match Made in Heaven *32*

Sister Scottie and the Beastie *35*

Sister Helga and the Antlers of Gluttony *38*

Sister Eleanor and her Invisible Brain *41*

Sister Madge's Damaged Alphabet *45*

Sister Ginger and the Cannibals *48*

Sister Nation and the Big Baby *51*

Sister Bertha and the Beard *54*

Sister Fifi and the Rude Teeth *57*

Sister Laurel and the Snuff *62*

Epilogue *65*

The Sister Madge Letters *67*

The Bumper Book of Nuns

Convents are religious places
Full of nuns with solemn faces
Praying loudly to the Lord;
Little wonder they get bored.
When the morning frost unfreezes
And they've had their chats with Jesus
Nuns of every shape and size
Love to play and socialise.

Scarecrow-tiggy, tunnel-ball,
Sisters love to play them all.
For, when all is said and done,
It's rather cool to be a nun.
Meet the nuns within these pages,
Some are silly, some outrageous,
Some are bad and some are good
And some have undies made from wood.

Quirky, perky, clever, comic,
Nuns whose tummies are atomic.
Gentle, mental, gay and hearty,
Naughty nuns who love to party.
Far too many nuns to mention
Waiting for your keen attention.
Step inside, my little ones!
It's *Sister Madge's Book of Nuns*!

Sister Madge Mappin

Sister Brock and Our Lady of Immense Proportions

Sister Brock, since she was six,
Loved dabbling with sticks and bricks
And reading hardware catalogues
(She fed her dollies to the dogs).

At convent school, in second grade,
She dreamt of the construction trade.
She asked her teacher, Sister Hilda,
'How do I become a builder?'

Sister Hilda's face went blue.
'That job's for boys, not girls like you.
Sit down, you little brat!' she said,
'And get that hard-hat off your head.'

But Brock said, 'Pooh!' and 'Get a grip!'
Left school for an apprenticeship.
By seven, she was banging nails,
By ten, constructing monorails.

Now nearby in that neighbourhood
Another creaky convent stood.
A crazy, crumbly, tumbly spot,
A place of beauty it was not.

And as the nuns walked to and fro,
They had to be on tippy-toe
Or else they'd plummet through the floor
And all the way to Singapore.

The convent leader, Mother Grace,
Was eager to rebuild the place.
But who could work such wizardry?
There came a voice, 'Let me! Let me!'

And there stood Brock in overalls,
With cranes and chains and wrecking-balls.
'I'll build a place that shines and stuns
With big wide rooms for big wide nuns.'

And build she did, with such great care,
A jolly folly in the air

With towers reaching to the sky;
It soon caught Sister Hilda's eye.

And green with envy was her face:
'This convent is a *lovely* place.
It really is a work of art,
The man who built it must be smart.

'I'd like to live here. Let me, please!
Which person should I ask for keys?'
The nuns all pointed straight to Brock
And Hilda's hair fell out with shock.

But Brock forgave her, nonetheless.
The convent was a huge success
With saunas, spas and waterslides
For all of Jesus' lucky brides.

Now Sister Brock has made her home
Inside the Vatican in Rome.
She's building there with love and zeal
A carport for the Pope-mobile.

Sister Flo and the Vegies

Sister Flo, a gardening freak,
Had quite a nasty shock last week.
While she was planting silver beet
A small voice cackled at her feet.

'Hey, droopy-drawers!' the voice began,
'Your bottom's bigger than Japan!
I'm over here, you dopey dill,
Down here beneath the window sill!'

'How dare you!' scolded Sister Flo.
'You cheeky little so-and-so!'
For she had only just found out
The speaker was a Brussels sprout.

It said, 'We've business to discuss!
Stop pouring that manure on us!
We don't enjoy it, not a bit.
Would *you* like getting soaked in it?'

A carrot by the garden gate
Said, 'It's the smell of it I hate.
You'd probably dislike it, too
If *we* poured jobbies over *you*!'

And all the vegies had a go
At nagging poor old Sister Flo.
When scolded by an artichoke
Her temper well and truly broke.

Potatoes, leeks, she dug the lot,
And stewed them in her cooking pot.
She baked a pastie, golden brown,
Said, 'Serves you right!' then wolfed it down.

Alas, the vegies got her back,
Flo suffered from a gas attack.
So noisy was her sorry plight
It kept the neighbours up all night.

Explosions rocked her small abode,
Her bathtub landed in the road.
Her toilet orbited the earth
And landed on a priest in Perth.

It happened just a week ago,
Now things have changed for Sister Flo.
When vegies to her rudely speak,
She simply turns the other cheek.

SISTER STEPHANIE AND THE GANG

The supermarket proved to be
A trial for Sister Stephanie.

'Oh rats!' she grumbled to herself,
'The birdseed's on the highest shelf.
Unless I gain some extra height
My Charlie won't get fed tonight.'

The manager, who lingered near,
Said, 'Having trouble, Sister dear?
Our shelves are much too high, you say?
Well, I see it a different way.

'The problem is, *you're* much too *small!*
A tiny speck, a ping-pong ball!
A monkey towers over you.
It's rather better looking, too.'

The little Sister left the store,
Returned with an almighty roar.
The windows smashed, alarm bells rang,
The nuns had formed a bikie gang.

The gang was fierce, the gang was mad,
The gang was hip and leather-clad,
With boots and beads and studs and spikes,
The nuns revved up their superbikes.

Then up and down the aisles they raced
From tissues to tomato paste.
'Yippee!' they cried, as piles of tins
Were scattered just like bowling pins.

They crushed the nuts, they blew away
The continental food display.

They squashed the squash, they split the peas,
They toppled all the toiletries.

The manager who'd been so rude
Was knocked into the frozen food
And there he lay in cold repose,
With two fish fingers up his nose.

The bikies rumbled home to tea,
Except for Sister Stephanie,
Who searched the smoking battleground
Until a pack of seed she found.

She paid the manager and smiled,
'I'm sorry that the girls ran wild
But really, you should not poke fun
At poor defenceless nuns, my son.'

Then off she roared upon her Harley,
Home to feed her vulture, Charlie.

Sister Bossy and the Angel

Sister Bossy always frowned
And bossed the other nuns around.

She often scolded Sister Mabel,
'Keep your elbows off the table!'
Then she picked on Sister Kimbo,
'Pull your pants up when you limbo!'

Sister Bossy in her den
Got quite a shock one evening when
An angel floated by her bed.
'I'm tuckered out!' the angel said.

'I can't stay long, I'm due at heaven
(God shuts the gate at half-past seven).
But look! I've torn my dressing-gown
And both my wings have broken down.

'I can't go back in such a state,
God's got a bouncer at the gate.
A mighty angel strong and stout.
You don't look nice, he chucks you out.

'So all I need,' the angel said,
'Is needle, thimble and some thread.'
But though the angel asked her nicely,
Sister Bossy answered icily:

'You are absolutely shocking
To enter bedrooms without knocking!
Worse still, you've moulted on my floor!
Out you go, mate! Out the door!'

Years later, Sister Bossy died
And up to heaven she did ride.
At heaven's gate an angel sat
Saying, 'Sister Bossy! Fancy that!

'Do you remember me at all?
I once paid you an urgent call.
I had to *walk* home, thanks to you,
A billion miles, and uphill too.

'Well, I've got news for you, my dear,
Now *I'm* the brand new bouncer here.
You think you're coming in? You're not!
You're going some place rather hot.'

The angel gestured with his wings.
'Buzz off,' he said, 'to Alice Springs!'
So don't be bossy, mark my verse,
You might end up in hell – or worse.

Sister Poppy and the Plague

Sister Poppy, God protect her,
Was a magazine collector.
Women's weeklies by the ton
Were hoarded by the frugal nun.

This silliness of Sister Poppy
Made the other Sisters stroppy.
'Burn those magazines!' they'd yell.
'They're filthy, mouldy and they *smell*!'

But nothing stopped the little hoarder,
Desperate measures were in order!
Late one night when she withdrew,
They flushed her weeklies down the loo.

Alas, the nuns were not to know
That things in sewers quickly grow.
Those women's weeklies multiplied
Through sewerage systems far and wide.

And when at last the time was ripe,
They burst from drain and waterpipe.
The country was awash with muck,
A women's weekly plague had struck!

Down every boulevard and road
A flood of women's weeklies flowed.
Pedestrians on shopping sprees
Were crushed to death by recipes.

And pictures of the latest frocks
And football players in their jocks
And movie stars with plastic smiles
And hairdos you could see for miles.

Now, Sister Poppy knew the mess
Was due to her, well more or less.
She hoped and prayed that it would rain
To make the country clean again.

Well, rain it did, I'm pleased to say,
The women's weeklies washed away.
'Thank God!' cried Poppy, much impressed.
And God replied, 'We do our best.'

Now Poppy's ways are not so weak,
She's still a women's weekly freak.
But, glory be to Sister Poppy!
She recycles every copy.

Sister Isobel and the Zoo

Our teacher, Sister Isobel,
Was kind and warm and sweet as well.

She had a heart of gold, it's true,
Last week she took us to the zoo.
We followed her in single file
Beside the cage marked CROCODILE.

And though it made a fearful din
When little Joseph toppled in,
Our loving Sister said a prayer
And tenderly she left him there.

Then when we reached the lion pit
Said Sister Isobel, 'Let's sit
And eat our picnic lunches here.
Be careful not to trip – *oh dear*!'

The giant pussies chewed and chewed
And that's how we lost Ermintrude.
'How sad!' said Sister. 'What a waste!
It's put me off my salmon paste.'

A cage of vultures next she spied,
'What pretty little birds!' she cried,
'You look as though you've starved for weeks!
Come Matthew, Daniel, pat their beaks!'

If Matthew hadn't panicked they
Would surely be alive today
But vultures can be nervous birds.
'You live and learn!' were Sister's words.

The next attractions on the bill
Were killer pythons from Brazil.
'I'll hold you up so you can see!'
Said Isobel. 'Whoops! Goodness me!'

And little Mary showed us all
How quickly killer pythons crawl.
In only half an hour or so
They'd wrapped her up from head to toe.

It soon was very clear to me
Our group had dwindled down to three:
Two kids (myself and brother Pete)
And Isobel, so kind and sweet.

'Oh look!' she cried. 'Some deadly fishes!'
Frankly, we were both suspicious
When she told the pair of us
To fetch our bathers from the bus.

So, just to keep our teacher cool,
We nudged her *splash!* into the pool.

And as she sank, said Pete my brother,
'One kind turn deserves another.'

Sister Christabel and the Cushion of Joy

Sister Christabel from Cooma
Had a raucous sense of humour.

Nothing gave her greater glee
Than things exploding in your tea
Or soap that made your hands turn blue
Or rubber rats and plastic poo.

The nuns despaired of Christabel,
Her silly little pranks as well.
They reckoned that their only hope
Was seeking guidance from the Pope.

They said to Him, in voices haughty,
'Sister Christabel is naughty,
Wicked wheezes bring her bliss.'
The Pope stood up: 'Now why is this?'

Said Christabel, 'I love to laugh,
We're far too serious by half.
If Sisters all wore smiling faces,
Convents would be joyful places.'

The Pope sat down with dignity
But I'm afraid He didn't see
The whoopee cushion on His chair.
I bet you know who put it there.

And what a noise the cushion made,
A rude and rasping serenade!
Although the nuns tried not to grin,
They couldn't hold their laughter in.

They wet their pants, they laughed like mad,
His Holiness was just as bad.
And as the tears rolled down His face,
Said Christabel, 'I rest my case.'

Now, thanks to Sister Christabel,
The nuns get on extremely well
And after morning exercise,
They practise chucking custard pies.

The Pope drops in from time to time
To join their merry pantomime

And, as a gesture of esteem,
He covers them in shaving cream.

Sister Joss and the Match Made in Heaven

Sister Joss loved outdoor sports
And knocking round on tennis courts,
And going off on five-mile runs
And playing with the other nuns.

Pyjama parties every night
And piggy-backs by candlelight.
It's not surprising in the end
That Joss was every Sister's friend.

But Mother Marge, the convent boss,
Was not impressed by Sister Joss.
She said her friendships were a vice,
And made her sit on blocks of ice.

She taunted her, 'You little cow,
You'll never get to heaven now!'
And that's when Joss resolved to go
To be a famous tennis pro.

The years went by and Joss became
An athlete of unrivalled fame.
And when she died, within a trice,
They welcomed her to paradise.

The angels grinned from ear to ear,
They all were dressed in tennis gear,
And Jossie couldn't help but laugh
When Jesus sought her autograph.

But Joss said, 'Mother Marge was clear,
She said I wouldn't make it here.'
And God responded, 'I'm in charge.
Now who on earth is Mother Marge?

'We haven't seen her round these parts,
For nasty folk with frozen hearts
Are something of a public menace.
Come!' said God. 'And let's play tennis.'

Sister Scottie and the Beastie

Beside Loch Ness a Scottish nun
Was walking in the noonday sun
When from the Loch a monster rose,
She trembled in her pantihose.

'I can't decide,' the monster said,
'To eat you up alive or dead
Or serve you on a bed of rice.
A nun pavlova might be nice.'

And while the monster ummed and erred
A timely miracle occurred.
Some lightning struck the monster Nessie
(Scotland never looked so messy).

Beastie bits from shore to shore –
The Sister fed them to the poor.

She's famous for the stuff today
(Her name's Macdonald, by the way).

Sister Helga and the Antlers of Gluttony

Sister Helga, Sweden's saviour,
Lived in Northern Scandinavia.
Skating comps and snowball fights
Were Helga's childhood delights.

But Helga had one vice, I fear.
She loved the taste of roasted deer.
Now, one or two would be okay,
But *she* ate seventeen a day.

A doctor told the greedy Swede,
'A change of diet's what you need.
Remaining deer are very few
And Santa wants a word with you!'

But Helga didn't heed his warning,
Went off hunting every morning.
Dasher, Dancer, Donner, Blitzen,
Ended up in Helga's kitchen.

One day Helga rose from bed
To find two antlers on her head.
Not dainty, tiny, little *twig*-ones –
Whopping great enormous *big*-ones.

Antlers on a deer look fine
But not upon a girl of nine.
In all the big department stores
They'd stick in the revolving doors.

But what made Helga most upset
Was going to the coin-laundrette.
When people saw her antlers high
They'd hang their britches there to dry.

Well, at the age of twenty-one,
She chose to be a Swedish nun.
She had a message to impart,
A simple one, and from the heart:

'Don't surrender to temptation!
Everything in moderation!
Never guzzle from the bottle!
Eat a little, not a lottle!'

Helga's now in ecstasy,
She has the angels round for tea.
Her special talent she exploits,
She dances while they all throw quoits.

Sister Eleanor and Her Invisible Brain

Sister Eleanor was dumb.
Her brain was tiny as a crumb,
She dined on cats and burning coals
And DVD remote controls.

She didn't dress like other nuns,
She wore balloons and currant buns,
An anchor chain around her hip,
Attached discreetly to a ship.

She'd scream her prayers to God in Greek
(A language which she couldn't speak).

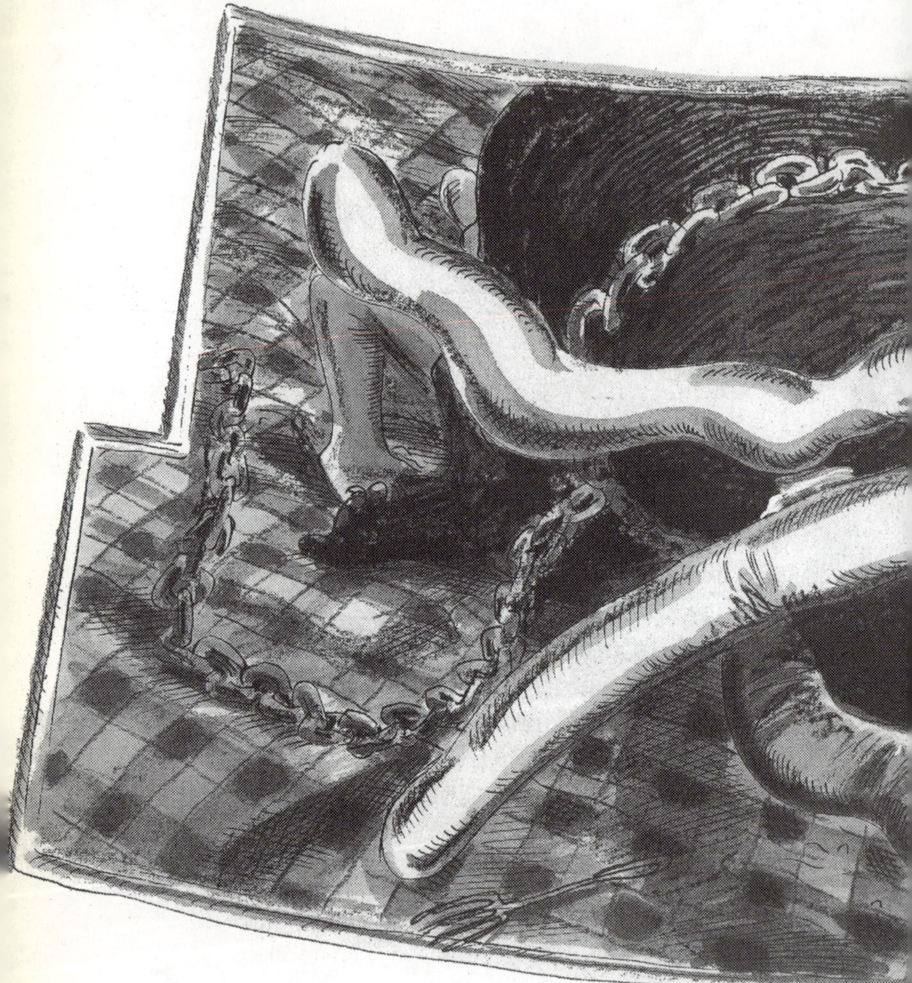

The only friend she ever made
Was half a jar of marmalade.

Yes, Sister Eleanor was dumb
And I'm afraid there's worse to come.
So thick and dense was Eleanor,
She thought that God approved of war.

And nothing you could say or do
Would make her think it wasn't true.
So now her twilight hours are spent
Advising Mr President.

Sister Madge's Damaged Alphabet

A is for apple, with black-and-white stripe

B is for boat, we eat when it's ripe

C is for carrot, a sailor's best friend

D is for dog, with sprouts out the end

E is for egg, that's shaggy all over

F is for frog, that we stick in pavlova

G is for God, that bounces away

H is for hairdo, to which we all pray

I is for igloo, on top of your head

J is for Jesus, an eskimo's shed

K is for kitten, that walks on the sea

L is for lion, as sweet as can be

M is for mother, with teeth that destroy

N is for nudist, that gives us all joy

O is for onion that doesn't wear pants

P is for pony (they eat them in France)

Q is for Queen, we ride to Dimboola

R is for rooster, our glorious ruler

S is for sandwich, that crows when it's light

T is for tigers, we all love to bite

U is for undies, that often attack

V is for vampires, that creep up your crack

W is for whiskers (we're frightened of those)

X is for x-rays, which come from your nose

Y is for you, revealing our bones

Z is for zebras, who read stupid poems.

Sister Ginger and the Cannibals

Upon a lonely grassy hill
Above the jungles of Brazil,
There lived a nun of utmost fame
And Sister Ginger was her name.

One night upon that fateful mound,
The cannibals were closing round
A-beating on their bongo drum,
NUN FOR DINNER! YUMMY-YUM!

Now Sister Ginger didn't want
To end up in a restaurant.
She prayed to God that she'd be saved
From being caught and microwaved.

So God replied, 'Don't worry, Sis!
I'll very soon take care of this!'
And as the natives neared her bed,
He stamped a message on her head.

The tribe surrendered with a bow,
'We won't eat Sister Ginger now.'
'Yippee!' she cried. 'But tell me, pray,
What *does* this wondrous message say?'

The natives moaned, their eyes were damp,
'God's given you a USE-BY stamp
And judging by the date we know,
You went off several weeks ago.'

But though the cannibals were foiled,
The little Sister's anger boiled.
'A USE-BY stamp? What utter gall!
Why, I'm the freshest nun of all!

'How dare that anyone suggest
My quality is not the best.
I'm no spring chicken, I agree,
But no one's out-of-dating me!'

Her foolish boasting cost her dear;
The natives ate her up, I fear.
In heaven, God looked down and sighed,
'So much for Sister Ginger's pride!

'It's better to be out-of-date,
Than fresh on someone's dinner plate.'

Sister Nation and the Big Baby

Scientific exploration
Was the joy of Sister Nation.
One strange potion she'd devised
Made Brussels sprouts grow cabbage-sized.

Just a dash from Nation's dropper
Turned a dwarf into a whopper.
What a shame that she forgot
To leave it in a nice safe spot.

One day, the Reverend snatched the brew,
He had a christening to do.
'The holy water's off,' he said,
'So this'll have to do instead.'

Well, can you guess what happened now?
He dropped it on the baby's brow.
The baby squealed, as babies do,
Then suddenly the baby *grew.*

He stretched until his nappy burst.
The people screamed, the Reverend cursed
And one old aunt, who stood alone,
Clucked, 'Oh, my goodness! How you've grown!'

I'm sad to say he sat on her
Then dribbled where the others were.
The Reverend said, as down it rained,
'I only hope he's toilet-trained!'

Of course, the noise and devastation
Soon attracted Sister Nation.
'Bad boy!' came her stern reproof
As baby's head went through the roof.

In desperate tones she cried, 'I think
That burping him will make him shrink!'
To carry out this bright idea
They slapped the giant baby's rear.

It took a dozen whacks before
The baby gave a mighty roar.
A burp so fierce, a burp so grand,
A cyclone swept across the land.

His burping done, the baby smiled,
Once more a small, contented child.
And, since the parents played along,
The Reverend christened him King Kong.

Now Sister Nation never leaves
Her potion in the path of thieves.
She markets it to movie stars
Who sprinkle it inside their bras.

Sister Bertha and the Beard

Sister Bertha had a beard.
The children thought that she was weird.
And all of them would stop and stare
For nuns with beards are rather rare.

Although she plucked it every night,
It grew straight back, a fearsome sight.
And didn't Sister Bertha hate it
When a walrus tried to date it!

Finally, she asked if God
Could tell her why she looked so odd.
And God responded, 'Yes, I can.
The fact is, Bertha, you're a man.

'It doesn't take a lot of sense
To tell the ladies from the gents.'
With that, Almighty God retired
And added, 'By the way, you're fired.'

Sister Fifi and the Rude Teeth

Sister Fifi dined on cakes
And sherbet bombs and jelly snakes.
Her diet was, without a doubt,
The reason that her teeth fell out.

A gummy nun, you'll all agree,
Is not a pretty sight to see.
So, to the dentist Fifi strayed
To have a set of dentures made.

And what a lovely set they were!
The nuns all chorused, 'Look at her!'
And Fifi's life was one big thrill
Until the dentist sent his bill.

'A thousand dollars!' cried the nun.
'You're joking! Pull the other one!
I won't pay that, for heaven's sake!'
And that was Fifi's big mistake.

The dental fairy called one night
And sprinkled Fifi's dentures bright.

Next morning when she popped them in,
Bewitchedly, they seemed to grin.

And then, to Fifi's great despair,
The naughty teeth began to swear.
They shouted, 'Cripes!' and 'Toilet roll!'
Her choppers were beyond control.

And when the Reverend chanced to come
Her dentures muttered, 'Bite your bum!'
A dreadful thing for them to do.
The Reverend bellowed, 'Same to you!'

A prayer to heaven Fifi gave:
'Oh God, please make my teeth behave!'
The answer came, 'Of course I will.
But first you have to pay your bill.'

Now Fifi always pays her debts,
She never grumbles or forgets.
And since that fateful day occurred,
Her dentures haven't said a word.

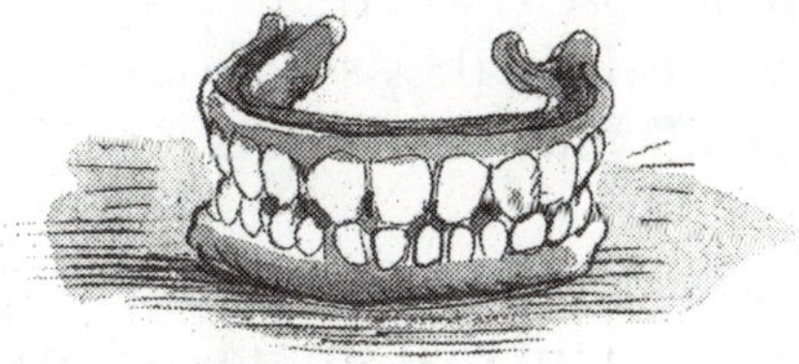

Sister Laurel and the Snuff

Sister Laurel, rough and tough,
Was very fond of taking snuff.
A stupid and disgusting craze
Which dates right back to olden days.

It's powdery and black like soot
And up your nose is where it's put.
Your nostrils twitch, they start to ache,
You sneeze till your suspenders break.

It's quite unsightly for a nun
But Laurel thought that snuff was fun.
In afternoon and evening prayer,
She'd sneeze completely everywhere.

The other nuns would all complain,
'That clot's been taking snuff again!
With all that rubbish up her snout,
She'll sneeze the stained-glass windows out!'

Alas, the nuns were quite correct,
The convent got completely wrecked.
The windows fell on Sister May
And Sister Bloom got blown away.

Their boss, whose name was Mother Rose,
Cried, 'Shove some cushions up her nose!
A mattress or a couch will do!
Just stop her crying out *Archoo*!'

Then, with a brilliant purple blast,
The sneezing Sister sneezed her last.
And all she left, God bless her soul,
Was one enormous, smoking hole.

This story has a simple moral:
Don't take snuff like Sister Laurel.
Noses should be quiet places,
Not volcanoes on your faces.

Amen

EPILOGUE

In the convent nuns are sleeping,
Hear their merry snores!
All except for one who's creeping
Through the library doors.
Who's that nun who sits and studies,
Quizzical and queer?
Yes, it's me, my little buddies,
Sister Madge is here.

While the rain outside is pelting
Over fields and cities,
Here I sit with candle melting,
Polishing my ditties.
If you've read my songs and snatches
And you think they're groovy,
Wait till you see *Sister Madge's*
Book of Nuns the Movie!

The Sister Madge Letters

The author would like to thank Dmetri Kakmi who patiently edited this special bumper version of *Sister Madge's Book of Nuns.* Poor Jane Covernton, who edited the original Omnibus edition, had a more difficult task. She had to work out whether or not Sister Madge was a real person.

Here are some excerpts of letters exchanged between Sister Madge and Jane Covernton, with one interjection by Doug MacLeod.

Dear Ms Covernton,
It has come to my attention that your publishing company is compiling an anthology of verse called Putrid Poems. *I am a nun and I believe I have a very keen sense of humour. The orphans are always laughing at the poems that I make up and recite to them.*
I enclose some of my work in the hope it may interest.
God bless you,
Madge Mappin (Sister)

Dear Sister Madge,
Thank you for the poems you sent us last week. My colleagues and I were thrilled to receive them and

are delighted to include them in our anthology. I must confess to being sorely tempted to turn one into a picture book. I would also like to know how you found out about our latest project.
Kind regards,
Jane Covernton (Publisher)

Dear Ms Covernton,
I'm so excited! I'm going to be in print!
I would love to write a book for you, pointing out how much fun it is to be a nun.
Some may claim having a book published will defy my vow of poverty but I can think of no better way of keeping it than by being an author.
God bless you,
Madge Mappin (Sister)
P.S. Writer Doug MacLeod mentioned your project when he came to speak to the orphans.

Dear Sister Madge,
Thank you for your enthusiastic response. We take your point about the vow of poverty and you may rest assured that you will not receive a penny from us.
Yours sincerely,
Jane Covernton (Publisher)

Dear Doug,
We can't thank you enough for putting Sister Madge on to us. I am sure we will be the envy of every publisher in Australia at having discovered yet another new author.

Meanwhile, when are we going to hear from you? We are a little disappointed that you have not submitted anything for our anthology to date.
Regards,
Jane Covernton (Publisher)

Dear Jane,
To be honest, I was dubious about referring Sister Madge to you. I was once invited to speak at her convent. She kept plying me with her silly rhymes. My advice to you is publish anything she writes.
With luck it might stop her pestering me.
Yours sincerely,
Doug MacLeod

Dear Doug,
Your game is up. You are a poet in nun's clothing. Our resident sleuth has matched the paper your letter was written on to the very same used by Sister Madge.
You will be paid a pittance for your scribblings of course; a just reward for your attempts to sabotage the good name of our publishing house and make us the laughing stock of the nation.
Yours sincerely,
Jane Covernton (Publisher)

Dear confused Ms Covernton,
I laughed my guts out when I read your letter (forwarded by Doug MacLeod). Your suggestion that Mr MacLeod and I

are one and the same person is absurd, as I am a much better writer.
God bless you,
Madge Mappin (Sister)

Dear Sister Madge,
I fear I owe you an apology. I did not believe you existed. I am now gravely aware of my error. It is the very least we can do to grant your every wish.
Yours sincerely,
Jane Covernton (Publisher)

P.S. Sister Madge, we've made out a cheque to you. In light of all that has passed we feel this is only correct.

About the Author

Doug MacLeod is a writer, TV producer and human.

Doug has worked on many of Australia's most popular TV shows, including 'Fast Forward', 'Big Girl's Blouse' and 'SeaChange'. He was also the executive producer on the three series of 'The Micallef Program' for the ABC, in which capacity he did nothing whatever.

He was head writer for the stupidly successful TV series 'The Comedy Company', and received many awards, including a perspex thing which got lost when his car was broken into.

Doug has also written a number of popular children's books. The original version of *Sister Madge's Book of Nuns* also won a few awards and he didn't lose any of them.

For the international charity, Comic Relief, Doug has written a new collection of funny verse, *On the Cards,* also illustrated by Craig Smith, to be published in October, 2002 by Puffin.

ABOUT THE ILLUSTRATOR

I have just been on the internet to find some information on Craig Smith. Craig runs one of the finest caravan showrooms in the world, in the state of Ohio in the USA. He offers great bargains on all caravan accessories and even has a refuelling station on site. Craig also offers excellent deals on new and second-hand travel-trailers and motor-homes.

What is most incredible is that Craig has achieved all this while being one of Australia's best-loved illustrators of children's books. He has won countless awards for his superb work on titles such as *The Birdsville Monster* and of course the original edition of *Sister Madge's Book of Nuns.* Some of Craig's other titles include *The Cabbage Patch Fib* and *The Cabbage Patch War* by Paul Jennings, the *I Hate Fridays* series by Rachel Flynn, and most recently Aussie Nibble *The Sandpit War* by Meredith Costain.

Actually, now I think about it, that stuff I got off the internet may be about a different Craig Smith. Although I'm sure the one who illustrated this book could sell caravans if he put his mind to it.

Anonymous

The Birdsville Monster

Doug MacLeod

Illustrated by Craig Smith

'Nurse Finkelstein and Dr Black
Were terrors of the Birdsville Track.
They both were ghoulish, gaunt and grim,
And she was twice the size of him.'

Tossed out of Birdsville for extremely naughty behaviour, Nurse Finkelstein and Dr Black want revenge. So they send Doug, their home-made monster, to scare the pants off everyone. But things don't go according to plan . . .

Get ready for the craziest outback adventure of your life!